Holding The Light

by

Jenna Plewes

First published 2024 by The Hedgehog Poetry Press,

5 Coppack House, Churchill Avenue, Clevedon. BS21 6QW

www.hedgehogpress.co.uk

Copyright © Jenna Plewes 2024

The right of Jenna Plewes to be identified as the author of this work has been asserted in accordance with the Copyright, Designs and Patents Act 1988. All rights reserved. No part of this publication may be reproduced, stored in or introduced into a retrieval system, or transmitted in any form, or by any means (electronic, mechanical, photocopying, recording or otherwise) without prior written permissions of the publisher. Any person who does any unauthorised act in relation to this publication may be liable for criminal prosecution and civil claims for damages.

ISBN: 978-1-916830-24-0

Contents

Wind dies at Sunset 7
Moth Holes in the Mind 8
Bric-a-brac of lost words 9
House Clearance 10
Engrained 11
Victorian Nursing Chair 12
Beechwood Corner Cabinet 13
Carved Ebony Statuette 14
Box with delicate brass keyhole 15
We regret we cannot replace the missing item 16
Framed Print 17
Stoneware Mug with a Blue Glaze 18
Do not Disturb 19

A snapper-up of unconsidered trifles

Autolycus A Winter's Tale

1
Wind dies at Sunset

Gentle the wild bird of your heart
    stroke its soft feathers

feel its pulse slow
    settle under your fingers

breathe stillness flowing through
    evening's wide windows

embers cool and soften   fade
    amber   abalone   ash

  woollen blankets heap the horizon
    purple darkens to slate

bats unstitch a silvery sky   darkness
    slips through the seams

the deep blue silence of the night folds
    around your soul.

2
Moth Holes in the Mind

Day after day she traces and retraces herself
        wading through gossamer,
                leaving a wake of broken threads
a thought floating
        on an updraft of association
                catches in a scramble of goosegrass

she unpicks sticky tendrils
        untangles handfuls of words
                tugs at the roots
                        the thought breaks

it wasn't always like this

threads were intricately woven
        gloriously coloured
            fine as spider silk
                rippled and shone
                    in the sunlight

now all that remains are shreds
                elusive memories
                            unravelling over fields of silence

3
Bric-a-brac of lost words

It's here somewhere; the word she wants
among the piles of memories sliding off shelves
spilling out of rucksacks and suitcases
dogeared scrapbooks and old diaries.

The will-o-the-wisp of her torch hovers over
a maze of footprints in the dust -   hers?
She's been here before, stumbled over it
whatever it is she's looking for.

It's here somewhere; the word she wants
she can smell it, like rain on baked ground
chew the muscle of it, taste salt, iron
it goes on ringing like a doorbell in an empty house.

She stumbles into the light, empty-handed.

The room hums to itself, shrugs deeper and deeper
into the dark.

4
House Clearance

A pic-a-stick pile of kitchen chairs
crumbling cliffs of tables, bedheads
wardrobes, chests of drawers
a trestle table of bric-a-brac
books, prints, cheap jewellery

here and there a shred of memory
a curl of baby hair in a tin with a picture of
Brighton pier on the lid, an envelope of photographs
a dog collar with a phone number on its battered disk

dust settles on a tray of medals
a pair of leather driving gloves, a shrimping net
box of tennis balls, garden fork and pruning shears

orphaned things, torn from their moorings
rummaged by ghosts.

5
Engrained

I smell of dough, shoe polish and engine oil
sticky with marmalade and homemade jam
I'm cup marked and wine stained, my body
scabbed with chewing gum, my legs
bruised and battered by muddy football boots.

I've been chewed by generations of puppies
dribbled on by babies, scribbled by toddlers
scarred with penknives and dinky cars
initialled in crayon and indelible ink
abused and extravagantly loved.

You could strip me to bare wood
oil and polish me until I shone like silk
but never scrub away the hugger-mugger stuff of
growing up and growing old, sharing secrets
arguing and making up, laughter, love and tears
sealed in my grain.

6
Victorian Nursing Chair

It's humiliating, a nightmare of prodding and poking
by rough male hands; upended, intimately examined
slack webbing, sagging button-back, chipped legs

balding rust-red velvet
smelling of dust and loneliness.

I was smooth satin, sweet milkiness of feeding
snuffle of drowsy contentment, lullabies

wide-lapped and low for little legs to scramble up
I've been a spaceship, magic carpet, trampoline

but

not every baby lived; not every toddler thrived;
there's weariness and grief soaked in my silence

clenched fists have pummelled me, screamed
in the safety of my lap, squeezed despair into my arms
stained me with tears, pushed me away.

Reupholstered

in my velvet years I reeked of hash and cigarettes
sodden in stale wine, I staggered under drunken sex

sagged under piles of books and magazines, legs clawed
by cats, chewed by an aging Labrador.

Now

harsh eyes study my provenance, pass judgement on
what they see, calculate what I am worth.

7
Beechwood Corner Cabinet

Sealed in my grain
the simmering of spring
sultry summer heat
autumn's glowing coals
winter's blown ash

my heartwood felt
the chew of chainsaw
bite of chisel, snug fit
of dovetail joint
bright sheen of wax

I was made for trinkets
for confidences
tucked in a corner

with secret drawers
for gossamer promises

cotton wishes
folded into squares

a third drawer
slim as a blade
held my heart
its key lost long ago.

8
Carved Ebony Statuette

Slant light from the table lamp
explores a calm impassive face
large eyes with heavy lids
lips sealed, thoughts buried deep.

I know this man, his warm voice
talked long into the night with him
walked Devon lanes, hand linked to his
I was 18, he was 25, studying law.

He offered me a road, a choice
to leave the land I knew, join
a nation forging its identity
factions surging like hormones.

Could I have shared his dreams
his bed, worn his wedding ring
grafted myself in him, borne fruit?

I hold the little statuette he carved
for me, heft the smooth nakedness
vulnerable black skin unblemished
remember that look of quiet certainty

wonder what became of him
and of that fledgling woman
teetering while he flew.

The country was Sierra Leone, and he was returning to the government

9
Box with delicate brass keyhole

This is the box that crossed an ocean
filled with hope and apprehension
fear and excitement, a box
with a key to a new life
tooled leather creased
as the smile on an ancient face

open the lid
           let out

years of sunshine and shade
           cottonwood trees in spring
campfire smoke and stars
           sticky fingers, marshmallow sticks
waffles and maple syrup
           scritch of skis on snow, skates on ice
sleepy children,
           moonlight and glow-worms

somewhere along the way
           the key was lost
laughter
    and tears
           spilled out
stories and memories
           jumbled together

the box is light
worn smooth
and warm with handling
close it gently
when the time comes.

10
We regret we cannot replace the missing item

Five topaz stones set in a small gold ring
blue as the sea on a summer's day, translucent
as a cloudless sky; a gift from you for no reason

except to make me happy; and it did; worn
under a glove while washing up, while gardening
living an ordinary, sunny life until, one day

a stone was gone, a window open to a darkening
sky, an unlatched porthole on a heavy-laden ship.

I probed the gap, a missing tooth, felt only brokenness
never saw the warning signs, felt the grip weakening
unclasping, falling away, until it was too late.

11
Framed Print

In another life
he could have been my grandfather
white hair and beard neatly trimmed
head bowed over steepled hands
as he gives thanks for his solitary meal.

A small loaf and bowl of soup is
all he needs, all he wants now.
The room is quiet and ordered
spectacles folded on the family bible.

If I opened it, would there be
births, marriages and deaths
carefully inscribed. Would I
find there the thread that tethers me

to who I am?

Darkness hides the corners of the room
he prays alone in the lamplight
while memories crouch in the shadows
waiting to pounce.

Grace by Rhoda Nyberg

12
Stoneware Mug with a Blue Glaze

Each week you offer me tea; a pause while the kettle boils
    you find the mug I claim as mine

the rounded breast of it, warmth cupped in my palms; a holding
    that lets me reach deep inside myself

where aloneness lies like a tarn, wild and brooding, blurred with
    scudding clouds and rain

a place of ghosts, regrets and unhealed hurts, of unacknowledged things
    lurking in the depths

I sip, swirl my thoughts, words stipple the surface, float, sink, dissolve
    minutes trickle like sand.

Glancing sunlight probes the room, kettle, teabags, box of tissues
    the hourglass run through, the cup empty.

13
Do not Disturb

tread quietly, this is where she's made her nest
two sagging easy chairs softened with cushions
newspapers scattered across a faded oriental rug

collapsing piles of books, a clutter of carrier bags
used teabags in a cracked jug, biscuit wrappers
two mugs on a coffee table, the clean one for visitors

a sugar bowl with a picture of Lyme Regis, matching
tin of tea. Two plates with a border of pansies, teaspoons
from Sidmouth, an open packet of custard creams.

The radio's thick with dust, she doses, nibbles a biscuit
crumbs fall on the floor. Sunlight filters through the nets
footsteps, click of the letter box, rustle of mail, she lifts

her head, half rises, then settles again among the cushions
smiles as the sun warms her face, closes her eyes. Tread
quietly, leave her there with her dreams, soft as feathers.

www.ingramcontent.com/pod-product-compliance
Lightning Source LLC
Chambersburg PA
CBHW020141130526
44590CB00041B/635